# POEMS and LYRICS
## for *My*
# CHILDREN

## VOLUME I

### Carol Laughingsong Carr

ISBN  979-8-9886705-0-6  (Hardback)
ISBN  979-8-9886705-1-3  (Paperback)
ISBN  979-8-9886705-2-0  (Ebook)

Printed in the United States of America

Enjoy the journey of teaching and learning with your children!

Train up a child in the way he should go… (Proverbs 22:6 KJV)
But be sure you go that way yourself. (Charles Spurgeon)

## Companion Music to Poems & Lyrics for My Children Vol I

Our Father's House publishing is thrilled to announce "*Songs* to Poems & Lyrics for My Children Vol I" the MUST HAVE companion music to the written work by Singer/Songwriter/Author Carol LaughingSong Carr - all ten professionally produced songs featured in the book are available for download on your favorite download or streaming service worldwide, (including   iTunes, Spotify, Amazon)

From tender melodies to rollicking reels to bittersweet airs, Carol's music offers an exciting interactive experience to accompany lessons, activities & singalongs for home school parents and teachers with children ages 3 - 9.
 Album includes:


* 10 songs written and performed by the author, (with a little help from her friends)
* + 4 spoken-word poems.

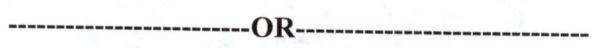

-----------------------OR---------------------------

**For savings on book and music bundles please SCAN the QRcode below to visit Our Father's House marketplace:**

# Contents

# Dear Reader, Teacher, and Parent

I have shared my poems and lyrics with children for generations.
I hope you can enjoy sharing and using these for yourself
and teaching others. I found teaching always helps us learn
along with our children. Flavia C. was a role model. As a Native
American, she was able to get only part of her elementary education.
As she reared her children, she learned along with them.

Flavia taught me to make the best of my circumstances.

Get Better, Not Bitter
Get better, not bitter when life hands you a lemon.
This world is so bitter the solution is to make it sweeter.
So let's make lemonade as our hurts fade into oblivion.
And go on and on to a sweeter future.
—Carol A. Carr

I hope that these poems and lyrics will bless many as
songs, lyrics, and nursery rhymes helped my children and me.

With much love, prayers, and blessings,

Carol Carr
Email: ourfathershouse.childlike736@aleeas.com

# Acknowledgements

I would like to thank those who inspired me to create.
Thank You, Father God, Jesus, and Holy Spirit for inspiring me!

My Family: Robin, Alene, Flavia, my son, and grandchildren.

Churches that allowed me to share poems and lyrics:
Rock Church, Broad Street Methodist Church, Liberty New
Testament Church, Colorado Community Church,
Old Country Church and New Hope and New Heart AG Church

Schools and Colleges: Portsmouth Public Schools,
Tidewater Community College, Norfolk State University,
Red Rocks Community College, Colorado

4

# Quiet as a Cat

shhhhhhhh

Quiet, please.

Walk quietly as a cat

tiptoeing.

Whisper only in my ear

as loud as a cat purring.

Work quietly as a cat

caring when someone

needs a catnap.

We can read a book

on our lap.

Parents and teachers can train their children when, why, and how to be quiet.
Genesis 2:1–3, God rests on seventh day.
Isaiah 11:6–9, Animals live peacefully.
Proverbs 6:6–8, Ants work wisely to supply their needs.
Ecclesiastes 5:12, We sleep well by working and not worrying.
1 Timothy 2:2, Christians are to work quietly. (See activity page.)

6

# Proverbs 31 Mom

My mom is a proverbs 31 mom.

My mom is a proverbs 31 mom.

I call her a blessing,

for she is always blessing me.

She gives warm clothes to me, to me.

She gives good food to me, to me.

She's always busy

taking care of me.

My mom takes care of me, of me.

My mom takes care of me, of me

I call her a blessing,

for she is always blessing me.

This poem is for Mother's Day. We paired up partners to do
clapping in 3/4 time. We made Mothers' Day cards
with this poem inside the cards. Proverbs 31. (See activity page.)

# Little Feet

Little coat,
little shoes,
little feet
that cannot reach the floor.
"Are we ever too little or too big?"

Little hearts,
little thoughts
with great feeling
reach out to our
heavenly Father.
"Are we ever too little or too big?"

Little hands,
little teaching,
little understanding
ask for the cup and the bread.
"Are we ever too little or too big?"

Although so little in our sight,
children like these
know His presence
and receive with happiness.
Children like these
run to him when he says,

"Let them come;
stand with me;
I'll lay hands on them
and pray blessings
over my little ones."

Are we too little or too big for Jesus to reach us where we are?
"Such is the kingdom of heaven!" Matthew 19:13–15

(See activity page.)

13

# Take This Staff

I will sing. I will sing.
I will sing over you with joy.
I will sing. I will sing.
I will sing over you with joy.

Take this staff in your hand, Adam.
Take this staff in your hand, Noah.
One day there'll be the Good Shepherd
Who will lead you home.
He'll take this staff into my land.
He'll take this staff into my land.

Take this staff in your hand, Abraham.
Take this staff in your hand, Isaac.
One day there'll be the Good Shepherd
Who will lead you home.
He'll take this staff into my land.
He'll take this staff into my land.

Take this staff in your hand, Jacob.
Take this staff in your hand, Joseph.
One day there'll be the Good Shepherd
Who will lead you home.
He'll take this staff into my land.
He'll take this staff into my land.

Take this staff in your hand, Moses.
Take this staff in your hand, Joshua.
One day there'll be the Good Shepherd
Who will lead you home.
He'll take this staff into my land.
He'll take this staff into my land.

Take this staff in your hand, David.
Take this staff in your hand, David.
One day there'll be the Good Shepherd
Who will lead you home.
He'll take this staff into my land.
He'll take this staff into my land.

Take this staff in your hand, my son.
Take this staff in your hand, my son.
Today you are the Good Shepherd,
Who will lead my children home.
Take this staff into my land.
Tell them, the kingdom of God is at hand.

(See activity page.)

# Because You Love Me

You love me within whether I lose or win.
It's the greatest love story
That has ever been,
Or will ever be
That you first loved me.
You went to Calvary's tree
Just to set me free.

Because you love me within
Whether I am the first or last
The best or the worst,
Or the greatest or the smallest.
You race to forgive my sins
Erase them as if they've never been,
Change my heart to love
That always wins.
Because you love me!

(See activity page.)

# Raindrops

If I were a raindrop.
I'd love the feeling,
The feeling to fly,
Fly through the sky.
I could look on
Farmlands,
Cities,
Oceans, rivers,
Mountains,
All in miniature.
As I'm hurling,
Faster and faster,
Closer and closer.
I would glisten, yes, glisten,
In the sunshine.

Fellow raindrops would,
Pitter, patter,
Pitter, patter,
Pitter, splatter,
On roofs.
All would become
Richer and richer,
Greener and greener.
Many a restless being
Would be listening and looking
At me just glistening
Until they would restTo
the pleasant
Sound of the symphony
Of drip, drop, drip, drop,
Pitter, patter, pitter, splatter,
Of landing raindrops.

So eased like inside
A cozy chair
Enjoying a curtain
That provides
A sound barrier
To the cares
Of this drop
In the bucket in the sky
Called planet earth.

(See activity page.)

# Son Shine

Daffodils, dandelions, clover all over,
Butter sun coming up over my shoulder.
Hubcaps on cars rolling down the street.
Top of the morning to you who leave sleep.
I open the car door for my friend the nurse.
I feel so happy just got to let love burst;
With laughing till pure divine love is all over.
Best son comes up over my shoulder.

You may think I'm full of daffy pills and dandy lines,
And I'm a silly young rover.
But Jesus's love makes burdens,
Go light, o light on my shoulder.
I feel so happy just got to let love burst,
With laughing till pure divine love is all over.
Best son comes up over my shoulder.

Yet I know, this world has ills not candy lions.
The way is praying over and over.
For Jesus's love makes burdens
Go light, O light on my shoulder.
I feel so happy just got to let love burst,
With laughing till pure divine love is all over.
Best son comes up over my shoulder.

Jesus tills with sure lines and grows love all over.
He changes fallow soil into gold sir.

"Son Shine" was written when I was nineteen years old and had arrived in Virginia in the springtime. The song was just a wondrous gift from my loving Father God. I had been carrying burdens during my childhood that I should not have had to bear. I felt Jesus lifting the burdens where my senses could enjoy all that is given in springtime. Matthew 11:28–30, Romans 8:34–35, Galatians 6:2.

(See activity page.)

# Rainbow Promise

Every time I see a rainbow in the clouds,
See the rainbow, see the rainbow, and see the rainbow.

I will look on it to remember my promise to you.
My promise, my promise, my promise to you.

My promise to you will always be,
All living on this earth:
Will live, will live, and will live.
Will live, will live, and will live.

During seed time and harvest,
Cold and heat,
Winter and summer,
Day and night:
Will live, will live, and will live.
Will live, will live, and will live.

That's my rainbow promise to you.
I want all to live, all to live:
Will live, will live, and will live.
Will live, will live, and will live.
My rainbow promise to you!

I wrote this for Noah and my class on September 14, 2003.
The children had fun waving banners of many colors and chanted the
repeated parts. Genesis 8:22, 9:11–17 (See the activity page.)

# Pumpkin Shine

Pumpkin, pumpkin, where are you?
I will find you in this pumpkin patch.
Pumpkin, pumpkin, I will pick you up,
Take you home and carve you a laugh,
While making a batch of pumpkin pie.

Pumpkin, pumpkin,
I will make your eyes,
And a big, big smile on your face.
Pumpkin, pumpkin, I will put a light,
Inside so you can dance with light.

Pumpkin, pumpkin, I will put you where?
Where you will not hide your light,
And all can see you shining bright.
Pumpkin, Pumpkin, Shine, Shine, Shine!

Jesus says: "Don't hide your light under a basket: let your light shine for all
to see."
Matthew 5:14–17 (KJV) I use this "dark day" to pass out tracts and,
pages to color and emphasize God's bountiful harvest season,
when children come to my door for candy.

(See activity page.)

30

# Four Seasons of Colorado

Dear Cody and Evan,
Summer is gone.
Fall has not left.
The harvest,
of pumpkins,
has just begun.
Snow fall has come before,
an October frost could color,
the leaves and let them all fall.
The snow sets the time for,
a winter wonderland to cover it all.

I have come inside to write to you;
So you can know,
When it snows in Colorado,
The buffalo has a big coat,
To keep them warm.
My coat is not as warm,
As his curly deep-brown coat.
Next spring, I can take off my coat fast,
While the buffalo cannot,
When it gets hot.

In Colorado summer, there are ice-cold streams,
Rushing fast down the mountain slopes.
Our rain sometimes has,
Quarter-size ice balls.

We are in the mile high city and,
A lot closer to the sun,
Which is like a magnifying glass,
That dries the streets of snow and hail,
Very fast in this highland dessert.
We get less rain, so we mow the grass less,
And rake the rocks more.

We have taller mountains,
More rocky cliffs,
Less green, and browner landscape,
Than the Blue Ridge Mountains,
in Virginia. At sunset sometimes,
Foothills of the Rocky Mountains,
Look like sleeping herds of giant buffalos.
These are the seasons of Colorado!

(See activity page.)

35

# If I Were Song

If I were a genius, a scientist, a scholar,
I'd teach you to be one, my son.
We could invent things useful to someone else.
We could make discoveries to solve problems.
We could develop theories to enlighten mankind.
If I were one, I surely would teach you, my son.

If I were a carpenter, and an electrician, a bricklayer,
I'd teach you to be one my son.
We could put up wooden frames that would be so sturdy.
We could put in wiring systems that were made safely.
We could build up walls that are straight and strong.
If I were one, I surely would teach you, my son.

If I were a policeman, a fireman, a doctor,
I'd teach you to be one, my son.
We could be strong and wise to protect others.
We could be brave and save people from fires.
We could work with God to heal our sisters and brothers.
If I were one, I surely would teach you, my son.

I sing this song when I'm feeling low inside.
It gives me hope one day I'll look on you with pride,
And you'll be something my son.
For maybe, I'm not such a smart person or greatly skilled.
Maybe I'm not strong or wise or as greatly talented as some.
Just maybe you'll be one, my son.

Since I am a poet, a composer and artist,
I'll teach you to be one, my son.
We can rhyme rhymes that tongues will love to ring.
We can write songs to dance to and sing.
We can create painting to stir the soul.
Since I am one, I will teach you these, my son.

(See activity page.)

38

# I Can Do All Things

Philippians 4:13 (KJV)
I can, I can, I can, I can,
Do all things through Christ,
Who strengthens me.
I can, I can, I can, I can,
Do all things through Christ,
Who strengthens me.

When my feelings are on the floor,
I can pick them up once more.
Because I can, I can, I can, I can,
Do all things through Christ,
Who strengthens me!
Who strengthens me!

I can see, I can hear, I can sing, I can believe,
To do all things through Christ,
Who strengthens me.
I can smell, I can taste, I can touch, I can tell,
To do all things through Christ,
Who strengthens me!

When my feelings are on the floor.
I can pick them up once more.
Because I can, I can, I can, I can,
Do all things through Christ,
Who strengthens me!
Who strengthens me!

I can, I can, I can, I can,
do all things through Christ,
who strengthens me.
I can, I can, I can, I can,
do all things through Christ,
who strengthens me.
who strengthens me.

(See activity page.)

42

# Think Twice

My God is so good and sweet,
He's loving kindness rolled,
In the Three in One.
He's sweeter than a honeybun.
Baked on a Sunday morn.

He teaches His daughters and His sons,
The secret of how it's to be done.
Loving kindness is one.
Loving kindness is in God's Son.

When people said mean things to Jesus,
He spoke truth in loving words.
He taught them loving kindness
He sang and taught:
I can see the love they've never been taught.
I can see the truth they've never been taught.

My God is so good and sweet,
He's loving kindness rolled,
In the Three in One.
He's sweeter than a honeybun,
Baked on a Sunday morn.

He teaches His daughters and His Sons,
The secret of how it's to be done.
Loving kindness is one.
Loving kindness is God's Son.

So think twice before you speak.
Make sure it's good and sweet.
Think twice before you do.
Make sure you want it to go back to you.

Speak truth in loving words.

(See activity page.)

# Activities and Lessons to Go with Poems and Songs

Quiet as a Cat. We made signs for the doorknobs with the poem and pictures. We played games to practice talking and walking quietly.
Say and model: Walk this way. Talk this way.
Read: Genesis 2:1–3, God rested on seventh day.
Isaiah 11:6–9, Animals live peacefully.
Proverbs 6:6–8, Ants are wise by working to supply their needs.
Ecclesiastes 5:12, We sleep well by working and not worrying.
1 Timothy 2:2, Christians encouraged to work quietly.

Proverb's 31 Mom is for Mother's Day. We had fun with partners to doing clapping in a 3/4 time Waltz. Also the poem is great for making Mother's Day Card. Read: Proverbs 31, How a mother cares of her family.

"Little Feet" Resources: pictures of Jesus, paper cups and plates, juice and bread to explain communion and praying blessings. Read: Matt. 19:13–15, Matt. 18:1–5, 10, Jesus took time to teach and pray blessings over children; and to have a humble teachable spirit (from Rabbi's Blessing).

"Take This Staff" Resources: walking stick to pass from child to child as they read or sing the lyrics. Talk about how many years and many shepherds until Jesus. Read: Matthew 1:1–17. God took generations for Messiah to come (from The Shepherd's Staff).

"Because You Love Me" teach under tree, have races (running, toy cars). Use blackboard to show how quickly God forgives and teaches us better ways. Read: John 3:16–17 and 1 Peter 2:24, Focus on Jesus paying and restoring us with His unconditional and sacrificial love.

Raindrops. Enjoy water play or learn about weather/science.
Read: James 5:17–18; 1 Kings 17:1 and 18:1 tell of word of the *Lord*
for Elijah to pray for rain to stop and to start raining again. Psalm147:8, God
and Creator of the Universe, He makes rain for the earth.

Son Shine. Good way to discuss and pray about burdens. Share stories
how God changes things for the better. Read: Matthew 11:28–30;
Romans 8:34–35. How Jesus prays and helps us bear our burdens.
Galatians 6:2 tells how we can help each other.

"The Rainbow Promise." Resources: use color paper or cloth banners or
scarves to wave to the poem/song while they chant the repeated
phrases. Grab hand full of crayons and use them together to draw a
rainbow. Genesis 8:20–22 and 9:8–14; teach what a
covenant and a promise is. Rainbow is sign in the sky of his promise.

"Pumpkin Shine." Churches and the Bible celebrates fall festivals and
God's creation. My grandparents shared donuts and apple cider with
their neighbors after harvest time. This day is an opportunity to *share
the Good News of Jesus with children* knocking on your door for candy
by giving Gospel tracts, coloring sheets and sharing songs and a puppet
show. On the "darkest day" *share the Gospel and let your light shine.*
Read: Matthew 5:14–16, Psalm 118:24, Leviticus 23:23–44.

"Four Season of Colorado." Enjoy God's creation and seasons with your
children. Take a nature walk, go to a botanical garden, visit a farm or
a zoo… Read: Genesis 1:1–14, God created day by day
and made the seasons. Ecclesiastes 3. There are seasons when
do or not do things. Psalm 147:15–18, He creates snow and hail.

"I Can Do All Things." Make homemade rhythm instruments out of cans, oatmeal boxes, cut up wooden dowels for rhythm sticks, fill containers with dried beans to make maracas. Philippians 4:1–13, Nehemiah 8:10.

"Think Twice." Make a sign or a poster with Think Twice or "What would Jesus do?" 1 Peter 2:22–24 (KJV). Jesus told no lies and reacted in and love. Psalm 19:7–11 The words in the Bible are more valuable than gold for we can learn to be wise, which makes our lives sweeter.

"At Heart's Door." We knocked on wooden pews when we sang this song. Could be fun to dance to also. Revelations 3:20 (from Healing in His Wings).

*Start a Good News Club* in your neighborhood at your house, church or after school activity. Offer tutoring in your church and have parents sign permission slips for children to participate in the Good News Club after tutoring.

*Tips*: Children learn multiple ways such as touching, seeing, hearing, crafting, and playing. All learn through pictures and objects, especially two- to five-year-olds. When children ask questions, it is a teachable moment. This book of *Poems and Lyrics for My Children* is a tool to Inspire nurturing, teaching and for you to find creative ways to share.

# Songs with Chords

# Little Feet

Intro [:CG:] C

1ˢᵗ verse

C                                                                                    G
Little coat, little shoes, little feet that cannot reach the floor.

                                                C  G
    "Are we ever too little or too big?"

2ⁿᵈ verse

C
Little hearts, little thoughts, with great feelings that can reach

                                        G
to the Heavenly Father.

                                                    C  G
    "Are we ever too little or too big?"

3ʳᵈ verse

C                                                             G                F
Little hands, little teaching, little understanding that asks

                                        C   G
for the cup and the bread.

                                                C  G
    "Are we ever too little or too big?"

4<sup>th</sup> verse

C                   G

Although so little in our sight children like these know

  C         G

His presence and receive with happiness.

F             C

Children like these run to Him when He says,

                  G

  "Let them come, stand next to me, lay my hands on them,

    F         C G

  and pray blessings over my little ones."

        C G          C

Are we ever too little or too big to let Jesus reach us where we are?

 C    F    G   C    F   G

"Such is the kingdom of heaven!" "Such is the kingdom of heaven!"

# Take This Staff

Intro AM DM G AM

```
AM                    DM              G                        AM
I WILL SING. I WILL SING. I WILL SING OVER YOU WITH JOY.
AM                    DM              G           E         AM  DM AM G AMI
WILL SING. I WILL SING. I WILL SING OVER YOU WITH JOY
```

1st verse
```
AM          DM                  G
TAKE THIS STAFF IN YOUR HAND ADAM.
AM          DM                  G
TAKE THIS STAFF IN YOUR HAND NOAH.
DM                                      G
ONE DAY THERE WILL BE A GOOD SHEPHERD
              AM    G    F
WHO WILL LEAD YOU HOME.
              DM        G              AM
2x [: HE'LL TAKE THIS STAFF INTO MY LAND! :]
```

2nd verse
```
AM          DM                  G
TAKE THIS STAFF IN YOUR HAND ABRAHAM.
AM          DM                  G
TAKE THIS STAFF IN YOUR HAND ISAAC.
DM                                  G
ONE DAY THERE WILL BE A GOOD SHEPHERD
              AM    G   F
WHO WILL LEAD YOU HOME.
              DM        G              AM
2x [ : HE'LL TAKE THIS STAFF INTO MY LAND! :]
```

3rd verse

```
AM         DM            G
TAKE THIS STAFF IN YOUR HAND JACOB.
AM         DM            G
TAKE THIS STAFF IN YOUR HAND JOSEPH.
DM                              G
ONE DAY THERE WILL BE A GOOD SHEPHERD
              AM   G   F
WHO WILL LEAD YOU HOME.
              DM        G              AM
2x [: HE'LL TAKE THIS STAFF INTO MY LAND! :]
```

4th verse

```
AM         DM            G
TAKE THIS STAFF IN YOUR HAND MOSES.
AM         DM            G
TAKE THIS STAFF IN YOUR HAND JOSHUA.
DM                              G
ONE DAY THERE WILL BE A GOOD SHEPHERD
              AM   G   F
WHO WILL LEAD YOU HOME.
              DM        G              AM
2x [: HE'LL TAKE THIS STAFF INTO MY LAND! :]
```

5th verse

```
AM         DM            G
TAKE THIS STAFF IN YOUR HAND DAVID.
AM         DM            G
TAKE THIS STAFF IN YOUR HAND DAVID.
DM                              G
ONE DAY THERE WILL BE A GOOD SHEPHERD
              AM   G   F
WHO WILL LEAD YOU HOME.
              DM        G              AM
2x [: HE'LL TAKE THIS STAFF INTO MY LAND! :]
```

6<sup>th</sup> verse

```
AM          DM                    G
TAKE THIS STAFF IN YOUR HAND, MY SON.
AM          DM                    G
TAKE THIS STAFF IN YOUR HAND, MY SON.
DM                               G
TODAY YOUR ARE THE GOOD SHEPHERD
                     AM    G    F
WHO WILL LEAD MY CHILDREN HOME.
                        DM       G       AM
TELL THEM, THE KINGDOM OF GOD IS AT HAND—!
AM                  DM         G                    AM
I WILL SING—. I WILL SING—. I WILL SING OVER YOU WITH JOY.
AM              DM        G      E      AM
I WILL SING—. I WILL SING—. I WILL SING OVER YOU WITH JOY.
```

# Because You Love Me

1st verse

```
G                                              C
You love me within whether I lose or win. It's the greatest love story
        D                      G
That has ever been, or will ever be you first loved me.
      C                          D
You went to Calvary's tree just to set me free.
```

2nd verse

```
                    G
Because you love me within whether I am the first or last
      C                        D
The best or the worst, or the greatest or the smallest.
        G
You race to forgive my sins, erase them as if they've never been,
C                                      D                  (repeat 1 and 2 verses)
And Change my heart to love that always wins.
        D        G      C        G
(end) Because you love me! Because you love me!
```

# Son Shine

Intro D G D A D G A D

1<sup>st</sup> verse

```
D              G           D            A
DAFFODILS, DANDELIONS, CLOVER ALL OVER,
D              G           A        D
BUTTER SUN COMING UP OVER MY SHOULDER.
D              G           D                A
HUDCAPS ON CARS ROLLING DOWN THE STREET.
D              G         A            D
TOP OF THE MORNING TO YOU WHO LEAVE SLEEP.
D                          G              D
I OPEN THE CAR DOOR FOR MY FRIEND THE NURSE.
           G           A             D
I FEEL SO HAPPY JUST GOT TO LET LOVE BURST;
                       G          D
WITH LAUGHING TILL PURE DIVINE LOVE IS ALL
A      D      G        A       D         G D A
OVER. BEST SON COMES UP OVER MY SHOULDER.
```

2<sup>nd</sup> verse

```
A                              D
YOU MAY THINK I'M FULL OF DAFFY PILLS AND
G                   D             A
DANDY LINES AND I'M A SILLY YOUNG ROVER
      D           G
BUT JESUS' LOVE MAKE BURDENS
```

```
            A                    D
GO LIGHT, O, LIGHT ON MY SHOULDER.
          G              A                    D
I FEEL SO HAPPY JUST GOT TO LET LOVE BURST
                        G          D          A
WITH LAUGHING TILL PURE DIVINE LOVE IS ALL OVER.
D        G        A        D          D G D A
BEST SON COMES UP OVER MY SHOULDER.
```

3rd verse
```
A      G A              D          G
YET I KNOW, THIS WORLD HAS ILLS NOT CANDY LIONS.
 D                              A
THE WAY IS PRAYING OVER AND OVER.
        D              G        A
FOR JESUS' LOVE MAKES BURDENS GO LIGHT,
                    D
O LIGHT ON MY SHOULDER.
D        G        A                D
I FEEL SO HAPPY JUST GOT TO LET LOVE BURST
                          G        D          A
WITH LAUGHING TILL PURE DIVINE LOVE IS ALL OVER.
D        G        A    D        D G A D
BEST SON COMES UP OVER MY SHOULDER.
```

Outro
```
D              G                    D          A
JESUS TILLS WITH SURE LINES AND GROWS LOVE ALL OVER.
        D              G        A    D
HE CHANGES FALLOW SOIL INTO GOLD SIR.
```

D G D A D G A D

# Rainbow Promise

1st verse

```
C                      F    G                C
EVERY TIME I SEE A RAINBOW IN THE CLOUDS,
                                          G    C
SEE THE RAINBOW, SEE THE RAINBOW, SEE THE RAINBOW!
                         F        G          C
I WILL LOOK ON IT TO REMEMBER MY PROMISE TO YOU.
                              G          C
MY PROMISE, MY PROMISE, MY PROMISE TO YOU!
```

2nd verse

```
C                  F    G   C
MY PROMISE TO YOU WILL ALWAYS BE
            F        G
ALL LIVING ON THIS EARTH:
        C              G C                        G C
WILL LIVE, WILL LIVE, WILL LIVE! WILL LIVE, WILL LIVE, WILL LIVE!
```

3rd verse

```
C                        F        G           C
DURING SEED TIME AND HARVEST, COLD AND HEAT
                    F              G
WINTER AND SUMMER, DAY AND NIGHT:
      C                  G C                    G C
WILL LIVE, WILL LIVE, WILL LIVE! WILL LIVE, WILL LIVE, WILL LIVE!
```

4th verse

```
C                        F        G
THAT'S MY RAINBOW PROMISE TO YOU.
   C              F          G
I WANT ALL TO LIVE, ALL TO LIVE:
      C                  G C                    G C
WILL LIVE, WILL LIVE, WILL LIVE! WILL LIVE, WILL LIVE, WILL LIVE!
                    G           C
MY RAINBOW PROMISE TO YOU!
```

# Pumpkin Shine

Intro Dm C G Dm

1<sup>st</sup> verse
```
Dm                    C   G   Dm
Pumpkin, pumpkin, where are you?
Dm                    C   G   Dm
I will find you in this pumpkin patch
Dm                      C   G Dm
Pumpkin, pumpkin, I will pick you up
D              C G D
Take you home and carve you a laugh
D                  C    G   D Dm
While making a batch of pumpkin pie.
```

2<sup>nd</sup> verse
```
Dm                      C   G   Dm
Pumpkin, pumpkin, I will make your eyes
Dm              C G  Dm
And a big, big smile on your face.
D                  C G D
Pumpkin, pumpkin, I will put a light.
                   C    G   D
Inside so you can dance with light.
```

3<sup>rd</sup> verse

Dm                           C   G   Dm
Pumpkin, pumpkin, I will put you where?
Dm              C  G    Dm
Where you will not hide your light
D              C  G  D
And all can see you shining bright.
D               C    G    D
Pumpkin, Pumpkin, Shine, Shine, Shine!
D               C    G     D
Pumpkin, Pumpkin, Shine, Shine, Shine!

Let your light shine !

# If I Were Song

1<sup>st</sup> verse

D                                                  G                      A

If I were a genius, a scientist, a scholar I'd teach you to be one my son.

            G                          D

We could invent things to be useful to someone else.

            G                     D

We could make discoveries to solve problems

            G                     D           A

We could develop theories to enlighten most of mankind.

C                    A                        D

If I were one I surely would teach you, my son.

2<sup>nd</sup> verse

D                                                  G                      A

If I were a carpenter, an electrician, a brick layer, I'd teach you to be one my son.

            G                          D

We could put up wooden frames that would be so sturdy.

            G                          D

We could put in wiring systems that were made safely.

            G                    D       A

We could build up walls that are straight and strong.

C                    A                        D

If I were one, I surely would teach you my son.

3<sup>rd</sup> verse

D                                                  G                      A

If I were a policeman, a fireman, a doctor, I'd teach you to be one my son.

            G                          D

We could be strong and wise to protect others.

```
          G                    D
We could be brave and save people from fires.
          G                    D              A
We could work with God to heal our sisters and brothers. Oh yeah.
C          A                       D
If I were one, I surely would teach you, my son.


Bridge [: Bm G C A :] BM
 Bm    G              C         A
I sing this song when I'm feeling low inside.
Bm      G            C              A
It gives me hope one day I'll look on you with pride
                        Bm  Bm
And you'll be something my son. For maybe,
              G           C    A
I'm not such a smart person or greatly skilled.
Bm          G            C              A
Maybe I'm not strong or wise or as greatly talented as some.
                        D
Just maybe you'll be one, my son.


4th verse
D                                  G              A
Since I am a poet, a composer an artist, I'll teach you to be one, my son.
          G                    D
We can rhyme rhymes that tongues will love to ring.
          G                D
We can write songs to dance to and sing.
          G           D    A
We can create painting to stir the soul.
C          A                   D
Since I am one, I will teach you these, my son.
(whistle, yodel, hum) D G A G D G D G D A D
```

# I Can Do All Things

Intro G C D G

1st verse
G
I CAN, I CAN, I CAN, I CAN DO ALL THINGS THROUGH CHRIST
     C        D     G     C
WHO STRENGTHENS ME. I CAN, I CAN, I CAN, I CAN
                             G
DO ALL THINGS THROUGH CHRIST WHO STRENGTHENS ME!

Chorus
G
WHEN MY FEELINGS ARE ON THE FLOOR.
I CAN PICK THEM UP ONCE MORE.

BECAUSE I CAN, I CAN, I CAN, I CAN DO
ALL THINGS THROUGH CHRIST
     C    D    G    C    D    G C D G C D G
WHO STRENGTHENS ME! WHO STRENGTHENS ME!

2nd verse
G
I CAN SEE, I CAN HEAR, I CAN SING, I CAN BELIEVE
TO DO ALL THINGS THROUGH CHRIST
     C    D    G    C
WHO STRENGTHENS ME. I CAN SMELL, I CAN TASTE, I CAN
TOUCH, I CAN TELL
                             G
TO DO ALL THINGS THROUGH CHRIST WHO STRENGTHENS ME!

Chorus
G
WHEN MY FEELINGS ARE ON THE FLOOR. I CAN PICK THEM
UP ONCE MORE.

BECAUSE I CAN, I CAN, I CAN, I CAN DO ALL THINGS THROUGH
CHRIST
       C        D    G     C       D       G
WHO STRENGTHENS ME! WHO STRENGTHENS ME!

G
I CAN, I CAN, I CAN, I CAN DO ALL THINGS THROUGH CHRIST
     C       D  G    C
WHO STRENGTHENS ME. I CAN, I CAN, I CAN, I CAN
                                       G
DO ALL THINGS THROUGH CHRIST WHO STRENGTHENS ME!

Chorus
G
WHEN MY FEELINGS ARE ON THE FLOOR. I CAN PICK THEM
UP ONCE MORE.

BECAUSE I CAN, I CAN, I CAN, I CAN DO ALL THINGS
THROUGHCHRIST
       C        D    G     C       D       G
WHO STRENGTHENS ME! WHO STRENGTHENS ME!
       C        D    G     C       D       G
WHO STRENGTHENS ME! WHO STRENGTHENS ME!

# Think Twice

Intro C F G C

1st verse

```
C                              F                         G
```
My God is so good and sweet He's loving kindness rolled three in one.
```
C                         F       G     C
```
He's sweet than a honey bun baked on a Sunday morn.

chorus
```
C            F       G      C          F      G    C
```
He teaches His daughters and His sons the secret how it's to be done.
```
          F     G C       F        G    C
```
Loving kindness is one. Loving kindness is in the Son.

2nd verse
```
C                              F            C            G
```
When people said mean thing to Jesus, He spoke truth in loving words.
```
      C                       F     G C
```
He taught them loving kindness. He sang and taught:
```
C        F       G       C
```
I can see the love they've never been taught.
```
C        F         G        C
```
I can see the truth they've never been taught.    Repeat 1st verse and chorus

3rd verse
```
C                              F          G
```
So think twice before you speak make sure it's good and sweet.
```
C                         F            G    C
```
Think twice before you do. Make sure you want it to go back to you.
```
      F      G C        F       G    C
```
Loving kindness is one. Loving kindness is in the Son.

# At Heart's Door

Intro: D/G/D/D/G/ D

1<sup>st</sup> verse

D                                                G                  D

Behold, I stand at the door and knock if anyone hears my voice

   D                         D       G     D

And opens the door I'll come into him and he with me.

        A   G     D        A   G     D

We will spend—the day feasting. We will spend—the day loving.

        A   G      D

We will spend—forever together my friend.

       G     A     D          G     A

And it's together forever together, And it's together, forever,

 D                            A  D

Together, forever, together, forever, A—men!

2<sup>nd</sup> verse

D                               G   D

E coute je me tiena la port et je frappe: si quel qu un entend

          G       D

me voix et ouvre la porte.

       A  G   D     A  G       D

J, entrerai—chez lui Je mangerai—avec lui

        A  G     D

Et il manger—avec, moi

G          A        D          G     A

Ensembler, tour jour, ensembler, esembler, tour jour,

D                                  A      D

Esembler tour jour, esembler tour jour, A—men!      Repeat 1<sup>st</sup> verse

# About the Author

Carol Carr was born in Washington, DC, February 1951 and grew up in the outskirts of that city until Randolph Junior High School in Maryland. She graduated from Cocoa High School in Florida and then much later went to Tidewater Community College where she obtained a welding certificate, associate of arts, a nursing assistant certificate in Virginia. She attended Norfolk State University studying music in Virginia and Red Rocks Community College studying theater in Colorado.

Her main passion is to serve in churches and ministries. She wants to share the journey she has had with her son, grandsons, and serving God in Sunday schools. This is what inspired and encourages her to take from some of her collection of poems and songs for you to enjoy. Carol hopes to publish her other songs, books, and musicals:

- The Shepherd's Staff
- The Rabbi's Blessing
- Healing in His Wings
- Mordechai's Dream
- Poems and lyrics for My Children Volume II